Life Is Better With You In It

A Little Book About Love And Life

Poetry by

Rodney James Dick

◆ FriesenPress

Suite 300 - 990 Fort St
Victoria, BC, V8V 3K2
Canada

www.friesenpress.com

ISBN
978-1-5255-7380-4 (Hardcover)
978-1-5255-7381-1 (Paperback)
978-1-5255-7382-8 (eBook)

1. POETRY

Distributed to the trade by The Ingram Book Company

A little about the author:

Hi there,

My name is Rodney Dick.

I was born and raised in the small town of Altona, in southern Manitoba.

Surrounded by friends and family, my youth and young adulthood was filled with love and loss (like many of you, I'm sure).

I hope you enjoy this book of simple poems, intended to be read (and hopefully related to) by one and all.

Several of the poems were written for, and inspired by, my best friend and soulmate (without whom none of this would have been possible).

Anonymous

Here's a poem about someone
A girl none of you know
She means more to me than anything
And I wanted to tell her so

She doesn't want any credit
"Anonymous" is her new name
She's not asking for any money
Nor is she seeking fame

I couldn't have done this without her
She gave me courage when I had none
If you asked who inspired my poems
I'd tell you that she's the one

She's my best friend and my partner
She's amazing in every way
When she asks if I think about her
I say "always and every day"

When we don't talk or text, I feel empty
Without her, I feel like I'm lost
I'd happily do anything for her
No matter what it might cost

She tells me that she's my number one fan
And she can't wait to buy my first book
To think it all started with a "tea date"
When deep into her eyes I looked

I could go on like this here forever
Telling you all how I feel
But the way it is, is simple
And it truly is quite surreal

From the bottom of my heart, I thank you
For standing beside me each day
You made me keep going forward
When stagnant I wanted to stay

But you lit a fire inside me
And you helped me make a fresh start
For that I am truly grateful
For that I give you my heart

I love you Anonymous

Time

Time is often not an ally
One on whom you can rely
Making you feel old and weak
Instead of young and spry

Often taking those we love
Far too soon it seems
Long before we got the chance
To live out all our dreams

Like a word once it's been spoken
You cannot get it back
Don't live your life filled with regret
Or longing or a lack

Love deeply and with passion
Be always strong and proud
Wear clothing not in fashion
Laugh often and laugh loud

Share a smile with a stranger
It's not real; it's just in your head
Forget about the danger
Before we know it, we'll all be dead

So live your life
Like there's no tomorrow
Don't waste it away
Filled with sadness or sorrow

Take a chance on life
Take a chance on love
Don't sit back and wish
On the stars up above

Do it for yourself
While you're still young and able
Get up off of the couch
Walk away from the table

It's ticking away
It doesn't cost you a dime
The one thing you can't buy
Is any more time

Longing and Lack

I only stayed a minute
It was all that I could do
I had to stop and visit
The last place where I saw you

Reminiscing is a pleasure
Wishing you were here to hold
All the times I truly treasure
And some of the stories told

I miss you, Mom, and I miss you, Dad
Thoughts of you are always on my mind
I miss you both, and it makes me sad
But your places of rest weren't too hard to find

I miss your smiles
I miss your laughs
In my favourite stories
You're the other halves

If you still have your family
Tell them you love them today
Don't let another day pass you by
And here are some words you should say:

I love you, I need you
To me you are the best
You can't call and tell them
After you lay them to rest

So, do it today
Say, "I love you guys"
Do it every day
Before it's goodbye

Because goodbye is forever
You can't get them back
What you can have forever
Is longing and lack

You

Which mask are you wearing?
Who are you deep inside?
You know just what I'm talking about:
It's the "you" you try to hide

You're afraid to let the world see
So you hide yourself in shame
Not wanting anyone to know
The real you ... or your real name

Stop hiding who you are
And who you want to be
Let your soul shine like a star
For all the world to see

Your soul is a hidden treasure
One that everyone should know
And the "you" inside you're hiding
Is the one that you should show

Don't pretend to be someone else
So that others think you're cool
Because when you are doing this
You're acting like the fool

Don't be ashamed of who you are
Or who you want to be
You are the "you" I want to know
But not the "you" I see

Lift your veil; take off your mask
Be proud of who "you" are
Because when you finally free yourself
You'll feel better off by far

Know That It's Okay

Some find peace in alcohol
Some find it in drugs
I find it in laughter
And giving awesome hugs

Hugs that say, "I love you"
Or "Man, it's been too long"
Just like the peace that you can find
When you hear a certain song

There's a feeling that you get
When you are holding someone near
And whispering softly, "I love you"
Right into a willing ear

It's really a feeling of true joy
Or one of total bliss
One that always seems to say
"It doesn't get better than this"

So, if you know somebody's struggling
Or they're having a hard time
Take a minute and hug them
'Cause it won't cost you a dime

But what it can do for them
Is turn their day around
You don't have to say anything
Or even make a sound

Wrap your arms around them
Hug and squeeze them tight
Look deeply right into their eyes
And say, "It will be alright"

Hug your friends and family
Know that it's okay
And if it's me you're seeing,
this is what I'll say:

"Know that I love you dearly, each and every day"

I Wonder If You'll Miss Me

I wonder if you'll miss me
When I'm dead and gone
Was there something that I did
Or said that was so wrong?

I've tried to give you everything
And do all I could do
So this distance I feel between us
Has got me so confused

What could I do better
As a parent or a friend
Other than just loving you
Until the very end?

I gave all of myself to you
That I thought I could
If there were something more to give
You know full well I would

The only thing you have to do
Is tell me what you need
And I will try to do it for you
Yes, I will indeed

I don't want to go through life
Without you by my side
These are feelings you know very well
Ones that I'll never hide

You know deep down inside your heart
That you mean the world to me
So tell me is there something more
That you need me to be?

When it's my time to leave this world
I wonder if you'll grieve
I wish you didn't hate me
This I need you to believe:

I've tried to be your father
Your guardian, and your friend
My love for you is infinite
For you there is no end

So please do me a favour
And remember me one day
As the guy who truly loved you
And who never walked away

As Bad As It Seems

He made a big mistake
When he left her that night
Not knowing what he'd be missing
As he walked out of sight

Forbidden love unexpected
Caught them both by surprise
The only thing that it took
Was one look in her eyes

Words were not needed
When he took her hand
Their hearts were united
With one look, but no plan

A road trip, a ride
A walk on the beach
A night in a cabin
True love within reach

Two hearts beating as one
A true love has been found
Not saying a word
Not making a sound

They made love through the night
Never seeming to tire
And lit up the sky
As if it were on fire

"If it's meant to be, it will be"
That's what some people say
But she had to leave
Though he begged her to stay

His heart is now hers
He gives all unto her
Every day for him now
Seems to be but a blur

What becomes of their love
that shines oh so bright
As they steal another kiss
Like two thieves in the night?

She quickly became his true love
And now, his best friend
Their tales still not written
At least not 'til "The End"

As each new day passes
He falls deeper in love
With this beautiful girl
Sent from Heaven above

His fantasy came true
Though too late, it may seem
The day he fell in love
With the girl of his dreams

Will she choose him
Leave the others behind
Or just stay where she is
And just keep him in mind?

Only time will tell
If their love's meant to be
All he can do now
Is just wait and see

He dreams of a day
When she sits by his side
Possibly one day
Becoming his bride

Don't give up hope
And keep chasing your dreams
Because life isn't always
As bad as it seems

My Best Friend

I use you as my sounding board
When I have things to figure out
You help me to believe in me
When I am filled with doubt

You support me in the things I do
When others walk away
You could've left me long ago
But you chose to stay

You led me through the darkness
And helped me see the light
You took everything that was wrong
And made it feel just right

Nothing can compare to you
No one can take your place
You are the reason for the smiles
Here on my heart and face

You're all I've ever wanted
My heart's yours until the end
And I just wanted you to know
That you are my best friend

You Are My Dream Come True

I searched my whole life over
Never sure for what or whom
But that changed in that one instant
When you walked into the room

Seeing you there before me
A beauty to behold
You brought light and warmth back to a heart
That had long been dark and cold

You make me feel so young
So careless, and again so free
You make me happier each day
Than I thought I'd ever be

Please believe me when I tell you
Because every word is true
That every song I hear these days
Reminds me more of you

Knowing that you're sad sometimes
Hurts like I've never felt
But when you share your smile with me
My heart begins to melt

Your kisses melt my butter
Your "I love you" melts my heart
My words I almost stutter
And I seem to fall apart

Every day and night together
I wish never had to end
Every day and night amazing
When enjoyed with my best friend

I had given up on love
I thought it was too late
Only to discover
My best friend and my soulmate

You know now that I love you babe
More than I can ever say
And I keep falling more in love
With you each passing day

Time is never ending
As is my love for you
I'd love to be beside you now
In everything you do

I hope I've made you smile
with my words of love for you
And now I'll tell you one more time
You are my dream come true

Alone but Not Alone

I knew what I wanted
Not a doubt was in my mind
But when I looked inside myself
Here's what I came to find:

Times change, and so do people
Best friends and lovers grow apart
And what it was you thought you felt
Has changed deep in your heart

You can be in the same room
"Together" but just not
So, it's time to take a good long look
And learn just what you've got

Do I stay here in this place
Unhappy where I am
Or do I leave it all behind
And form another plan?

I don't want to start all over
It's scary on my own
Leaving everything behind
And making a new home

I know it can be hard to do
When you're alone and feeling lost
But you have to do it for yourself
No matter what the cost

You deserve just to be happy
And should settle for nothing less
You know exactly what to do
So don't doubt or second guess

What others think about you
Are their thoughts, and not your own
So it's best to leave it all behind
When you're alone, but not alone

Perfect

Seeing you after all these years
Has done something to me
It's brought back a flood of emotions
Like a ship sailing out at sea

Your eyes, your walk, your laugh, your talk
Not a thing has changed
You're as beautiful as ever
And my love for you remains

You took me completely by surprise
When I saw you right before my eyes
I see you happy (as you should be)
But now I wish you were with me

Life has dealt me a funny hand
That has brought me back to you
Back to a girl of whom I've dreamed
With feelings strong and true

You know my thoughts and deepest desires
Seeing you again has re-lit the fires
The fires that burned so long ago
Now have me yearning for you so

But I have to leave, and you have to stay
And now all I can do is hope for the day
The day that I hold you tight in my arms
And protect you, as mine, from any harm

You're perfect and amazing
You're the girl of all my dreams
I missed out on love, long ago
Though recent it still seems

Our futures are uncertain
Being sadly still unwritten
But I just wanted you to know
With you, I am deeply smitten

Perhaps ... one day
I will be your man
And we'll walk through this life
Side by side, hand in hand

This poem isn't perfect
But that's what you are to me
I love you very much my friend
And what will be, will be

Loved Ones Lost

It's not often that I'm lost for words
And I find these hard to say
But I really miss my parents
Each and every single day

I've also lost two brothers
And several friends down here on earth
I hope that in the afterlife
They understand their worth

Why do I have to mourn them
And carry all these pains
When all of my fond memories
And love for them remains?

A song can cue a memory
That makes me start to cry
The thought that often echoes
Haunting me each time, is "Why?"

Each of them was so young
And they were all so good
Why can't they be here with me
Just exactly as they should?

Some advice I offer here
It's right from me to you
It's a very simple thing
That you should simply do

If there's someone out there
Whom you deeply care about
Pick up the phone and call them
Why not give them a shout?

We all may never understand
The fundamental cost
Or pain that we will surely feel
Because of loved ones lost

Stepping Up

I didn't help in your creation
But you truly helped in mine
Making me a better person
Than the one I left behind

"Stepping up" was unexpected
When you showed up my life
But oh, what a feeling it gave me
Far more happiness than strife

Mom, Dad, or my first name
It doesn't matter what you call me
Because of you, I'll always try
To be the best I can be

You are now my children
And you have all my heart
It matters not at all to me
Just where you got your start

Adopted, step, or foster child
No limits on my love for you
You make me smile and drive me wild
No matter what you do

You're my girl, my boy, my pride and joy
You are all I could ask for
Because of you I know that I
Will never want for more

My love for you remains undying
I'm here for you no matter what
Stole my heart without even trying
No ifs ... no ands ... no buts

My heart is yours
Until the end of time
I love you dear
Sweet child of mine

Starting Over

It's not always easy
It's harder than you thought
It took you by surprise
And that's when you got caught

Caught up in the moment
Taking life for granted
Not watering the garden
Or the seeds you planted

Suddenly they're gone
And now you feel their lack
What could you do different?
What would you take back?

Did you do enough
With the time that you had?
Did you make them feel happy
Or did you make them feel sad?

If you know you did your best
Then that is all that matters
If you think about it all too much
You'll get sadder and sadder

Know in your heart
That you did your best
Take your negative thoughts
And lay them all to rest

Give yourself the time to heal
And your heart time to mend
When the winds of change blow
Don't break ... just bend

Take it all in stride
Know you'll be okay
Now cherish every moment
Of each and every day

You've got people around you
With hearts you did touch
No matter your struggles
They love you so much

Reach out and take a hand
To help pull you through
Because we all love you
It's the least we can do

Cherish yourself
Like a rare four-leaf clover
And know it's not easy
When you're starting over

My Heroes Are My Kids

Everyone's got someone
Who's inspired them to change
Someone whose life meant more than their own
It's really not that strange

Who's your inspiration?
Who's your guiding light?
Who is it that you think of
When you go to sleep at night?

Your life changed for the better
From the choices that you made
Because before they came to you
You didn't make the grade

You were nothing special
At least that's how you felt
Until the day they came to you
And your heart began to melt

You watch them as they're sleeping
Just lying in their beds
As you sit in wonder
What goes on inside their heads

How do they feel about you?
Were you good enough?
Were you far too lazy?
Were you far too tough?

Then one day they're all grown up
It took you by surprise
It seemed to happen overnight
Right before your eyes

They're no longer babies
They're amazing young adults
You hope that when they think of you
They forget about your faults

Mine gave me cards for Father's Day
And told me how I did
That is why I'm here to say
"My heroes are my kids"

The things they said about me
Had me crying tears of joy
They'll always be my little girl
And my little boy

So, who is it that changed you
And made you be your best?
I leave it up to you right now
To figure out the rest

It's really not that difficult
For you to do your part
Just take the ones that you hold dear
And love them with all your heart

Friendship

Friendship is a funny thing
That can last for many years
It can be filled with laughter
And also filled with tears

Cherish every moment
And everyone you know
Once they are gone, they're gone for good
So I hope you told them so

Don't fear the words "I love you"
Say them often; say them loud
Don't hide your true emotions
Of them all you should be proud

Remember these few words my friends
You're blessings in my eyes
If I haven't told you recently
I truly love you guys

Forget About the Hate

I'm more than just the image
Of the person that I see
When I'm looking in the mirror
And I'm looking back at me

I've got a mind, a heart, and soul
And they make me complete
I'm a member of the human race
And we cannot be beat

We're not all that different
All of us down here on earth
So stop and think about that
When you consider another's worth

Sadly, I am often judged
By what's outside, not in
Or hated by some others
For the colour of my skin

I might speak a different language
That you might not understand
This is not my first home
I am from a different land

That doesn't make you better
Or your hatred of me right
I only want to be at peace
When I go to sleep at night

You don't even know me
Why are you projecting hate?
Before you say or do it
Just stop, it's not too late

Now, if you read this poem
And you think you can relate
Remember to show love and just
Forget about the hate

From Out of Nowhere

It started off so simple
Innocent and fun
But the moment that he saw her
He knew she was the one

Their eyes met first, and quickly
And then they began to glow
And the crush that they'd once felt
Soon began to grow

They shared a hug for the first time
And he really wanted to kiss her
He didn't know at that moment
Just how much that he would miss her

They texted and talked for the next few days
And quickly fell in love
It was almost as if some magical force
Was giving them a shove

The feelings that they both soon felt
Took them by surprise
But what an amazing feeling it was
Getting lost in each other's eyes

She planned a trip to see him
Even though they'd never kissed
And standing there beside the lake
They found out what they'd missed

A kiss so filled with passion
Was the first one that they shared
There had been nothing quite like it
And no one else compared

She was all that he'd imagined
He hoped it would never end
Not only had he found true love
He'd also found his best friend

His heart belongs to her now
It's hers to keep forever
He needs for this amazing girl
To know he'll leave her never

He didn't think he'd love again
Or still had love to share
He was surprised to have it fall
From out of nowhere

Life

This life is far from perfect
It's harder than it seems
Plugging along on the road of life
With broken hearts and broken dreams

Don't give up
Don't give in
You're stronger than you know
Every little setback is there to help you grow

You've got your friends and family
To help along the way
Know that we all love you
And our love is here to stay

It's going to get better
You're going to be fine
If you need a shoulder
You're welcome to use mine

Chase your dreams and catch them
Make those babies real
Every wound you've suffered
With time will surely heal

These words are meant for everyone
Who's ever been in doubt
If you ever need me
I'm here to help you out

My love is unconditional
It's yours, no strings attached
Call me anytime you need
For you, there is no catch

I Believe in Me

Who do you believe in?
Unto your own self be true
If you really want something in life
It's totally up to you

Dismiss all of your worries
And forget all of your cares
No one can do it for you
Because it's your dream, not theirs

Think about it daily
Create the image in your mind
Then live like you already have it
And soon "it" you will find

It can come to you quite quickly
And take you by surprise
If you see it in your mind
You will soon see it with your eyes

We all get discouraged
And have our share of doubt
So don't give up on yourself
Or just sit down there and pout

You'll have it when you're ready
When you believe it, it comes true
It's not because of someone else
It's completely up to you

You can have all that you want in life
And be all you want to be
When you look into the mirror
And say, "I believe in me"

Because of You

I wasn't quite expecting this
It caught me by surprise
I fell deeply in love with you
With one look in your eyes

Your energy is magnetic
Your smile beautiful too
But what it was that did me in
Your eyes so deep and blue

You have my heart completely
It's yours to do with as you will
Your love is like a wonder drug
A magical little pill

I cannot get enough of you
There are not enough hours in the day
For me to tell you how I feel
Or what I'd like to say

When you picked the song you'd like to hear
As you're walking down the aisle
You should've seen my eyes light up
Or the way I began to smile

Knowing that you share my dreams
With you being my wife
Has me visualizing the future
And our long and happy life

Filled with laughter and with love
As happy as can be
I'd love to tell the world each day
How much you mean to me

I'm feeling like a teenager
As giddy as can be
Glowing from the inside out
For all the world to see

I gave you once a simple gift
A keychain with a key
To represent my love for you
And what you mean to me

It is the key to my home
And it's also to my heart
It represents a life of love
I hope we soon can start

I once was often lonely
Often feeling sad and blue
But that no longer is the case
And that's because of you

Choices

Some can be so easy
While others are so hard
Made on a roll of the dice
Or the turning of a card

They can change life in an instant
Though you thought you'd thought it through
When you made the choice it seemed
The right thing that you should do

Life is all about choices
Am I right, or am I wrong?
Do I continue to stay where I am
Even though I don't belong?

What's the worst thing that could happen?
Things don't work out the way you thought
Instead you chose to settle
And that's when you got caught

Caught up in a life
That isn't right for me
Stuck in a place
I do not want to be

I could drag this out forever
And never choose to act
Pretending that the life I had
Will somehow stay intact

It's time to make some changes
Listening to my inner voice
And start living out the life I want
Because it is my choice

I refuse to settle
Or let a moment pass me by
And fill my life with more regrets
Because I'm too afraid to try

Join me in the journey
Finding pleasure at every turn
And experience the lessons
That life wants us to learn

Our futures aren't guaranteed
Take a risk and take a chance
Join me out here on the floor
Come join me in the dance

Imagination

Close your eyes and let it take you
On a magical little trip
Let it take you through the heavens
On your flying ship

Let it dance to the rhythms
Deep inside your mind
Let it lead you off to treasures
You thought you'd never find

Unlock your deepest desires
As your dreams start to unfold
Imagine with me, if you will
That you'll never grow old

You're spending time with loved ones
And you're loving every minute
Of the dream you dream inside your mind
And all those with you in it

Nothing holds you back in this world
As it does in your real life
You have no times of trouble
And you have no times of strife

Limitations don't exist
Not inside this place
In your mind, you can jump and play
And always win the race

Reality is often
A place I like to leave
I need a place where I can go
To find my own reprieve

A place I can escape to
That has no limitations
I'm thankful I have this wonderful thing
We call imagination

Don't Give Up

We all know someone who knows someone
Who had pain and couldn't bear it
They might still be here with us
Had they taken the time to share it

Don't hide your pain from others
Share your struggles with a friend
And know that, with a little help
It'll be better in the end

We all feel pain and suffer loss
We've got the scars to prove it
If something's standing in your way
Call me, I'll help you move it

Don't be ashamed to ask for help
That's what we're all here for
If you think that you've tried hard enough
Just try a little more

It isn't always easy
This thing that we call life
It can be filled with times of joy
Or filled with times of strife

Take a look around you
Try to see what you can't see
What do you think that you would do
If I were you, and you were me?

I hope you'd want to help me
And do the best you can
To figure out just what is wrong
And come up with a plan

A plan to make it better
And let you know you're not alone
Just come on over to my place
Or call me on the phone

The answers lie within us
Even when they're hard to find
Don't be afraid to ask for help
I assure you; I don't mind

Your friends and family love you
And we don't have a choice
There's only no one there for you
If you don't use your voice

I've been too late to help someone
Who saw just an empty cup
And that is why I'm begging you
Please ... don't give up

Dreamers and Doers

I've always been a dreamer
And never been a doer
Because when you are a dreamer
The disappointments are much fewer

Dreaming is so easy
Because there's nothing for you to lose
You can sit there and do nothing
If that is what you choose

You dream of "what if one day"
Or "wouldn't it be nice"
But never even take a chance
Or think about it twice

You don't depend on others
Only counting on yourself
And all too often, you take those dreams
And put them on a shelf

A shelf where they sit dormant
And never come to light
Because you thought they weren't worth it
And didn't want to fight

Don't take your dreams and flush them
Long forgotten down the sewers
Make them your reality...

That's the difference between dreamers and doers

Don't Stand Behind the Curtain

All we really have is now
Not yesterday or tomorrow
Don't live your life filled with regret
Or fill your days with sorrow

Enjoy each present moment
As if it were your last
Not hoping for a better time
Or dwelling on the past

Make today your best day
Filled with laughter, smiles, and glee
And try to find the beauty there
In all the things you see

If you love them, tell them
If it's meant to, it will be
If you sit back and do nothing
Then nothing is all you'll see

Precious moments are fleeting
They never seem to last
Why is it that all the good things
Always seem to go too fast?

Take a chance to lose at love
And risk your heart being broken
Don't walk away from your soulmate
Or leave those words unspoken

If you do, they might meet someone
Who had the nerve and took the chance
And now that lucky someone
Gets to dance your dance

So, if now is all there ever is
And the future is uncertain
When you're up there on the stage of life
Don't stand behind the curtain

Time to Care

We all came from energy
We all came from a source
No matter what you call it
We've got an inner driving force

Whether you believe we evolved from monkeys
Or the oceans and the seas
Or were created from a god above
If that is what you please

One common trait we all have
Is that we share imagination
About our own beginnings
Or the thing some call creation

I'm not sure what to call it
Or what it is that I believe
But there has to be something more
When it's my spirit's time to leave

I'd love to see my family
That left me way too soon
Or take a trip across the sky
And fly around the moon

I am nobody special
I'm just a normal guy
Who'd like to meet some people
Who have brought tears to my eye

To meet some famous authors
As well as spiritual leaders
And tell them it's because of them
I became an avid reader

Or meet some great philosophers
Some artists, and some poets
And thank them all for taking the time
To learn their skill and show it

Some of us never realize
What it is that we can share
I'll end this with some simple words:
Just take the time to care

Which Door Would You Choose?

Suppose you were given a choice
To change some things you've done
Would you choose to go back in time
And try to have more fun?

Or would you stay right where you are
Because you're happy with what you've got
Even though you know to some
It's really not a lot?

You've got great friends and family
And you're happy with who you are
Even though you're not a millionaire
Or driving an exotic car

I think of these things often
Yet I know just what I'd do
Because if I changed anything
I might lose all of you

I wouldn't have my kids
Who've brightened up my every day
And helped make me a better man
Than I was yesterday

Some friends they might be gone as well
Who helped me through tough times
And it's because of their characters
I chose them as friends of mine

I'd lose so many memories
Ones I cherish to this day
Like holding onto my father's hand
The moment he passed away

Or when my son came into this world
And opened his eyes the very first time
That one, I can assure you
Is a favourite one of mine

The universe brings you what you think of
Whether you want it to or not
So be careful what you wish for
Or you might lose all that you've got

Every choice you make in life
Creates something you could lose
So, be careful when you ask yourself
Which door would you choose?

There's No Place Like Home

We all came from somewhere
We all call one place home
It matters not where you are from
Or how far that you roam

Whether it's a village
A town or a big city
To forget where you are from
Would be such a great pity

It's a place filled with childhood memories
The kind you'll never forget
Or maybe you're still living there
And you haven't made them yet

Perhaps where you met your best friend
Or the place where you first fell in love
Made a wish upon a shooting star
Or got your first ball and glove

Where you learned how to ride a bicycle
Or drove your very first car
It's the place where you made some mistakes
The ones that made you who you are

It doesn't matter where you started
Or how far you choose to roam
The one thing I've discovered
Is that there's no place like home

You Don't Know the Real Me

We talk about a lot of things
I guess that much is true
But we're always holding something back
Because it's what we do

Not everything is easy
To talk about these days
So we tend to keep some things inside
Because it's just our way

Either we're too embarrassed
Or too ashamed to share it all
We'd rather keep some things inside
So we're alone here when we fall

We don't want to take you with us
To this place here in the dark
Sharing only all the brighter things
Just like sunshine in a park

Please do not get angry
If we don't let you in
Some days it is just really hard
To live inside this skin

Don't blame yourself for struggles
That you didn't know about
It's not your fault you didn't know
It was us who kept you out

We smile on the outside
Because that's what you want to see
I guess that's just another reason why
You don't know the real me

Treasures

Sitting here in silence
Lost inside my mind
Searching through the memories
Of treasures I might find

Some seem like only yesterday
Yet decades have gone by
Memories of another time
That often make me cry

Friends will come and friends will go
These things we know for certain
Don't sit back in your chair of life
Peaking from behind the curtain

Witness dreams
Live life first-hand
Believe in love
And take a stand

Share of yourself
Your thoughts and your dreams
This thing called life
Goes by quickly it seems

Before you know it
Your time is at hand
And it's time for you
To leave this land

I love this life
And all of you in it
So close your eyes
And think for a minute

How could I be better?
What more could I do
If I could get a second chance
To be a better friend to you?

I'd make up for lost time
And live life with no regret
Cherishing every moment ...
On that much you can bet

I'll cherish you always
And in my heart, you'll stay
If I could ask just one thing:
Please, don't ever go away

I hope you know I'm here for you
All hours, day or night
And that I've always got your back
No matter what the fight

Knowing you has always been
A deep and honest pleasure
And your friendship is a lovely gift
That I'll always treasure

Follow Your Bliss

People all too often stay
In a place they don't belong
They feel they're being selfish
Or that leaving would be wrong

Not necessarily a physical place
It can be a place inside your mind
So if you look inside yourself
Here's what I hope you'll find

Don't let grief or assumed guilt punish you
Being happy is your God-given right
It shouldn't be a struggle
Nor should it be a fight

You can be, do, and have all you want in life
All you have to do is ask
Then realize that you're worthy
And put the universe to task

Don't stay somewhere unhappy
Or lose yourself in the deep, dark abyss
Nor settle for less than you deserve
Always follow your bliss

Anxiety Is Evil

I don't suffer with it
But I know a few who do
And this is my interpretation
Of what they're going through

Hiding in the darkness
Afraid to face the light
Not wanting to be seen
So you only go out at night

You lock yourself away
And keep the world outside
It's not due to shyness
Nor is it lack of pride

There are fewer people out there
With the midnight hour at hand
So that's when you feel the safest
To roam about the land

You don't want anyone to see you
You don't want to say a word
You feel like you'd be better off
To not be seen or heard

You're not sure when it started
Or, for that matter, how
All you know is that it's happening
And it's happening right now

It's a fear that just takes over
One you wish you could explain
So someone else could understand
And help you through the pain

Anxiety is evil
It's wicked and unfair
Just know that I am here for you
Because I love you, and I care

Bring Them Back

I remember a time
Not so long ago
When someone you met
Became someone you know

When a beautiful girl
Could walk down the street
And not be afraid
Of whom she might meet

A time when children
Would play outside until dark
And you weren't afraid
To walk through the park

When service was given
Above what was paid
And people took pride
In the things that they made

Respect was given
To one and to all
It didn't matter their age
Nor how big or how small

Honor and integrity
Meant something back then
When one's word and a handshake
Sealed a deal between men

Oh, how I miss
Those simple things that we lack
And what I would give ...
To just bring them back

Life Gets in The Way

So many plans
And so much to do
The hours in a day
All too often, too few

Visions of yourself
In a much better place
Get pushed back in line
No matter your pace

Things you meant to do
Now sit there and wait
And you're hoping when you're done
That it's not too late

Too late for your dreams
Finally to come true
All simply because
There was too much to do

There is no magic wand
And there's no magic pill
That can slow down time
Or make it stand still

Try to be just like Santa
Make a list, check it twice
And don't worry whether
You've been naughty or nice

Give yourself a break
Every once in a while
And do something for "you"
That just makes your heart smile

Don't wait until you're old
And your hair has turned grey
It happens so fast
When life gets in the way

Fix Yourself First

If you could make things better
Where is it that you'd start?
Would you fix the things around you
Or deep inside your heart?

We tend to look outside ourselves
When things are going wrong
Often times forgetting
That we can't always be strong

Asking for assistance
Doesn't mean you are weak
I think it shows that you are strong
When someone else's help you seek

Stop trying to do everything
Let another share your load
If you keep trying to do it all
You might feel like you'll explode

Remember ... it's important ...
Before things go from bad to worse
Don't be ashamed to ask for help
And always fix yourself first

About the Author

Rodney James Dick (better known to his friends and family as "Bugsy") was born and raised in Altona, Manitoba and currently lives in Victoria, British Columbia, Canada, in a two-bedroom apartment overlooking the ocean (one of the many places he finds inspiration for his writings).

CPSIA information can be obtained
at www.ICGtesting.com
Printed in the USA
LVHW090215071220
673499LV00004B/37

9 781525 573804